THE POUND HILL MOB

Titles in the Harvestime **High Adventure** series:
River in Flood — Peggy Burns
Secret of the Driftwood Elephant — Peggy Burns
The Pound Hill Mob — Mark Jeffery

A video version of *The Pound Hill Mob* has been produced by CVG Television and can be hired from leading video hire centres. In case of difficulty, or if you wish to purchase a copy, contact: CVG Television, Unit 7, Forge Wood Estate, Crawley, Sussex RH10 2PG, or: Harvestime Services Ltd, 136 Hall Lane, Bradford, West Yorkshire BD4 7DG

THE POUND HILL MOB

Mark Jeffery

Illustrations: Tim Lovell

Harvestime

Published in the United Kingdom by:
Harvestime Services Ltd, 136 Hall Lane,
Bradford, West Yorkshire BD4 7DG

First published by Harvestime
First printed March 1988

British Library Cataloguing in Publication Data

Jeffery, Mark
The Pound Hill mob
I. *Title* II. *Lovell, Tim* III. *Series*
823'.914 [J]

ISBN 0-947714-56-1

Typeset by: Ocean Typesetting,
Headingley, Leeds, West Yorkshire

Printed and bound in the United Kingdom by:
Richard Clay Ltd, Bungay, Suffolk

Contents

For Diana and our own Pound Hill Mob:
Luke, David, Daniel, Benjamin, Seth, Leah-Maarit

The new girl

1

It was the start of the new term at Pound Hill Middle School.

For most kids it was just a case of new classroom, new teacher. Otherwise, it was the same old routine. You know it well. Registration. Into assembly.

'Good morning, school.'

'*Good morning,* Mr *Hawtin.*'

Have you all had a good holiday?'

'*Yes,* Mr *Hawtin.*'

But not everybody was bored by the routine. For Elaine, it was all new. Elaine had moved to Pound Hill eight weeks ago at the end of the summer term, but this was her first day at the new school.

Nobody had seen Elaine before, not even during the long summer holidays. She had been assigned to Miss Morris's class for no other reason than there were fewer girls in 4M.

Miss Morris had read with interest the report from Elaine's previous school: '*Elaine is a quiet, unassuming girl. She lacks confidence but has a warm and genuine personality.'*

Of course, the trouble with starting the autumn term in the first week of September is that it's sometimes the warmest week of the whole summer; in fact, this year it was the only really hot week of the year.

So when the final bell rang, everybody made a bolt for the school door and fresh air.

4M were first in the scramble to get to the front of the queue at the water fountain.

For Michael Jones, the rush was unnecessary. He always had a can of Coca-Cola for morning break and Dr Pepper for after school. Not for him the squabbles and fights to quench his thirst.

One other feature marked Michael out from the rest of the kids — his 200-gram bar of Cadbury's Dairy Milk chocolate. This indulgence probably contributed significantly to his obvious weight problem.

On this particular day, Michael was leaning against the toilet wall nibbling into the third square of his C.D.M. when the new girl, Elaine, slowly walked by, head down and looking thoughtful.

Michael turned to Andy, who had decided to help him prop up the toilet wall, and said, 'What's the new girl's name?'

'Elaine Beni-something,' Andy replied in his usually helpful manner.

'She looks a right wally!' added Michael with emphasis.

'She's just come to live down at Foxgrove somewhere,' volunteered Andy, as if Michael's last comment was lost on him.

But Michael hadn't finished yet. 'She makes ET look human,' he concluded.

'I heard that, Michael Jones.' It was Emma. Emma was as different from Michael as chalk from cheese, and she certainly wasn't going to let him get away with that kind of attitude.

'Actually, she's quite nice. She sits opposite me in class.'

'Typical girls,' muttered Michael under his breath.

As Elaine continued on, avoiding the struggles at the fountain by walking round the playground instead of across it, she heard someone calling her name. She turned and saw Netsie running towards her, telling her to wait. Netsie was a friend of Emma's and the three of them sat at the same table in class.

'Where are you going?' asked Netsie, slightly out of breath.

'Oh, just for a walk till the bus comes,' Elaine replied, without stopping.

Not to be put off, Netsie kept up with her. 'I'll come, too,' she said. There was an awkward silence. 'Do you like the school?' asked Netsie, trying to get the conversation going.

'Yes, it's not bad,' Elaine mumbled. Then, realising the impression she was making, she smiled and added, 'Well, it's quite nice really.' But remembering the events of the morning she added, 'It's just . . . well . . . that boy Michael's been so nasty.'

'Oh, he's not so bad, really,' said Netsie, trying to cheer her up. 'It's just that he's been spoilt at home and thinks too much of himself.'

As Elaine made no reply, Netsie changed the subject. 'Hey, why don't you come home with me tomorrow after school and I'll show you my new stereo?'

Elaine blushed in embarrassment for no apparent reason. 'No thanks, I've just remembered something,' she replied quickly, almost without thinking.

She spun around to head back to the school, and suddenly bumped into Michael, who was following close behind with Andy.

'Ouch, my foot!' shouted Michael in exaggerated pain. 'I've got new shoes on!' he went on. And then, to really make his point, said, 'Just 'cos you got yours from a jumble sale!'

Even Andy was taken aback by this unprovoked attack. 'That's a bit much, Michael. You've really upset her now.'

Emma joined in: 'I don't know why we put up with you.' She gritted her teeth with contempt.

To save what could have been a heated argument, Claire arrived on the scene. She'd just passed Elaine going in the opposite direction. Claire had smiled and said, 'Hello,' but had got no response from her, other than a faint smile.

Now she guessed that something had happened between Netsie, Emma and Michael. You could cut the atmosphere with a knife.

'What's wrong with Elaine?' asked Claire.

'I'll give you one guess.' Netsie sounded exasperated.

'Not Michael — again!' Claire moaned emphatically.

Not to be outdone, Michael mimicked Claire's voice, 'Not Michael — again!'

This was too much for Netsie. 'Ignore him and he might go away,' she said angrily.

Having disposed of Michael, the girls attempted to have a serious conversation.

Claire started. 'I asked Elaine to come over on Saturday morning and she got very upset and walked away.'

'That's funny,' Netsie frowned, 'I just asked her to come to my place tomorrow. That's what started it all off.'

Suddenly, all conversation was interrupted by the dramatic arrival of Mark Wilson on his bike. Mark and his BMX were a continual hazard to the inhabitants of Pound Hill as he practised his 'instant braking technique'.

Not achieving his usual amazed reaction, he joked, 'Cheer up, everybody, it might never happen.'

Still no reaction. 'All right, what's up?' he asked reluctantly.

'It's Elaine, the new girl,' answered Netsie seriously.

'She's been acting very funny,' added Emma.

'She *is* funny!' That was Michael again, of course.

'Shut up for a minute!' said Claire angrily. Then, to the others, 'Netsie and I both invited her home and she just walked away — all sad-looking.'

Mark now became serious. 'I noticed nobody seemed to talk to her except us in the gang.'

'I'm sure there's something wrong,' said Emma.

An idea dawned in Mark's mind. 'I know. After school tomorrow let's all walk home with her. Then we can tell her about the gang. Perhaps she'd be happier if she knew we were all friendly.'

Everyone agreed that this would be a good move.

Michael, however, had other things on his mind. 'Well, you lot can stand around talking all you like but if I don't get going I'll miss my tea and then there'll be a stink.'

'Michael has such a way with words,' commented Netsie as they all dashed off in different directions.

2

When Miss Morris arrived the next day to collect her books for marking, she was surprised to see Elaine working at her desk during the lunch-hour.

She smiled warmly and approached Elaine's desk. 'How are you settling in, Elaine?' she asked.

'Oh, all right, thanks,' Elaine replied. Then, as if by way of explanation, she added, 'I just thought I'd stay in and finish my homework instead of doing it at home tonight.'

This was a cue for Miss Morris, who had spent some time talking to Elaine's mother on the phone the previous afternoon.

'How are things at home?' she asked. 'I know your mother's anxious that you should make some friends.'

'Well, I have to get home early in the evenings, but . . . .'

Elaine was interrupted by a crash at the classroom door as Michael came dashing in, pursued by Andy, who tripped and knocked Michael, who in turn spilled his textbooks all over the classroom floor.

Miss Morris was cross at being so rudely interrupted. 'Michael Jones, how often have I told you not to run in the school? If I find you running once more, you'll get a detention.'

Michael continued picking up his books with great embarrassment.

'Yes, miss,' he replied apologetically.

'Sorry, miss.' added Andy, more explicitly.

'You don't behave this way at home, so why do it at school?' Miss Morris added, not wanting to let them off the hook too easily.

'Sorry, miss,' Andy repeated.

By now Michael was totally distracted by the sight of the class gerbil playing in its cage. The little mouse-like creature was scurrying to and fro with athletic delight.

Michael was intrigued. A question sprang from his lips: 'Can we feed the gerbil, miss?'

What could 'miss' say? She agreed. 'But be careful,' she warned. At least if the boys could be kept out of mischief she could talk quietly to Elaine.

Miss Morris offered to show her the library, which would be a relatively quiet place to work in.

As soon as they'd gone through the door, Michael dived for the cage.

'There's not much gerbil food left,' commented Andy.

'Well, it ain't having any of my chocolate, that's for sure,' insisted Michael, opening the lid of the cage and putting his hand in.

'You'd better not let him escape,' warned Andy. 'Remember last time. It was found three days later in the girls' toilets.'

'Yeah. Claire almost went berserk!' Michael put a handful of grains in the feeding-bowl and tried to stroke the flighty creature, but gave up and fastened the lid again.

Andy wandered over to have a look at Elaine's work in more detail, as she had left it on her desk. He was impressed, pointing out that Elaine had done over five pages of work during the morning.

Michael condescended to look but was unimpressed. 'I bet Netsie helped her,' he said.

'She doesn't say very much, does she?' continued Andy.

Suddenly, Michael came up with one of his brainwaves. 'I've just had a brilliant idea of getting some life out of her,' he announced. 'This'll really wake her up.'

Andy watched as Michael took Elaine's shoulder-bag, unzipped it and rummaged inside. He found what he was looking for, Elaine's lunch-box, and put it on the desk, flipping open the catch.

Taking out a pair of sandwiches wrapped in cling film, he handed them to Andy. 'Put these on the teacher's desk a minute,' he ordered.

'You're not going to hide her packed lunch are you? She'll be starving this afternoon,' said Andy, putting two and two together and making five.

Michael was undaunted. 'Don't be stupid. I've got a much better idea than that. The gerbil!' He raised his eyebrows knowingly.

Andy was becoming nervous. 'Whatever you're going to do, Michael, I'm having nothing to do with it. You're always going a bit too far lately.'

But Michael wasn't going to be diverted, not now. 'You wait. It's only a joke. It'll be a good laugh,' he said all at once.

Andy just stood there, unsure what to do. Michael was becoming impatient. 'Hurry up and give me the lunch-box,' he pleaded. 'Come on.'

'All right,' agreed Andy reluctantly, bringing him the box. Opening the cage once again, Michael picked up the gerbil by the tail. 'Come on. There's a good boy,' he encouraged the little creature.

He dropped it into the plastic lunch-box and closed the lid in such a way that it wasn't airtight. 'Now stay in there and keep quiet,' he told the gerbil.

Voices were approaching along the corridor.

Michael took a quick step back from the table just as Emma and Elaine arrived through the door.

Emma noticed something was up by Michael's face. Seeing Elaine's lunch-box on the desk and the smirk on Michael's face, she was suspicious and interrogated him.

'Michael, have you touched Elaine's lunch-box?'

Michael just stared back at her with a look that said, 'Who? Me?'

It was like a red rag to a bull. Emma was furious. 'We all know you're the youngest in the class, but you ought to grow up a bit.'

Elaine, concerned about her meal, opened the box. Immediately, out popped the gerbil, dashed across the desk and dived down on to the floor. The two girls screamed and jumped up on chairs.

'Watch out!' laughed Michael, 'He'll bite your leg off.' This was more fun than he'd thought.

Meanwhile, the gerbil had dashed to the far end of the room.

'Michael, catch it quick,' shouted Andy, now concerned.

The two boys got on their hands and knees and tried to retrieve the elusive gerbil. But the creature was too fast. Every time they reached out for it, it bolted.

Emma was pleased to see their struggles. 'I hope you get into trouble,' she scoffed. 'It's about time someone sorted you out.'

After several more unsuccessful attempts, the inevitable happened. The door opened and in walked Miss Morris. Michael looked up to see her standing over him.

'What's happening here?' she asked crossly.

'Shut the door, miss. Quick,' screamed Emma. The teacher obeyed instinctively. 'Michael let the gerbil out,' Emma was pleased to say.

Miss Morris was exasperated. 'Michael, I told you to be careful.' Michael gave a helpless shrug. 'Stand back,' she said. 'Where is it?'

'Over there,' pointed out Michael. 'It'll probably come to you, miss.' Michael was ever the optimist.

Ignoring him, the teacher ordered everyone to form a semicircle and make slowly for the corner of the room until the gerbil was cornered. When it tried to make a dash for it, one of them was sure to catch it.

Eventually, the gerbil did indeed make a dash, straight to Michael, who grabbed in vain. 'It slipped through my fingers, miss,' was his pathetic excuse.

The group re-formed and headed for another corner.

This time Miss Morris made sure she grabbed the gerbil herself, which she did by cupping her hands around its body. She slapped it into the cage and closed the lid before it had another chance to escape.

'So, how did this happen?' Miss Morris asked. Everyone looked at Michael. 'Yes,' she sighed, 'only you could have done something like this.'

'He did it deliberately, miss,' said Emma, determined to see the guilty punished. 'He put it in Elaine's lunch-box *and* he took her sandwiches.'

Elaine was embarrassed by all the drama. 'It's all right. Don't worry about it.'

But Miss Morris *was* worried. 'Where is Elaine's

lunch?' she asked Michael in her sternest voice.

'It's on your table, miss. I was going to give it back to her,' Michael continued as innocently as possible. 'The gerbil was a joke, miss. I didn't mean it to escape. I would have put it back. I won't do it again. I've learnt my lesson. Honest.'

'Have you finished, Michael?' asked Miss Morris.

'Yes, miss,' smiled Michael, thinking he had convinced her.

'Right,' she continued, 'you can do detention next Thursday afternoon. And I don't want to see either of you boys in here again until the end of term.'

'But, miss,' protested Andy at his own innocence, 'it wasn't . . . .'

'Go on. Both of you. Out!' she interrupted.

They shuffled slowly. Michael turned back. 'Out!' she shouted to hurry them along.

'Cheers, Michael,' said Andy dejectedly as they headed up the corridor. 'You get everyone in trouble. If this carries on the way it's going, you'll have to leave the gang.'

Michael was depressed. 'I don't know why things always have to go wrong for me.'

3

Thursday afternoon came and the gang all made for the school gate ready to intercept Elaine.

Andy spotted her first, coming across the yard all alone, head down. 'Hey, everybody, Elaine's coming.' They tried to look relaxed and put on their broadest smiles.

'Hello, Elaine,' piped up Netsie. Without waiting for a reply, she continued, 'This is our gang. You've met most of them already, I think. This is Mark, our newly-elected leader.'

'By one vote,' chipped in Michael.

'And how many votes did *you* get?' fumed Claire, determined to put him in his place, whereupon which Michael sank his teeth into two more squares of chocolate bar.

Not to be distracted, Netsie continued, 'We thought we'd walk home with you tonight and tell you about our clubhouse and . . . .'

Elaine, suddenly animated, butted in. 'No . . . . No, I'm sorry. You can't. I'm sorry . . . . Bye.' In near panic, she hurried off.

'Curiouser and curiouser,' said Andy blankly.

'That's who she reminds me of . . . the white rabbit,' chirped Michael without undue effort.

The rest of the gang tactfully ignored this last remark and boarded the school bus in silence.

* * *

Magnolia Cottage was about three-and-a-half miles from Pound Hill School and at least one mile past the housing estate where most of the gang lived.

The house was surrounded by trees and shrubs so that the untidy state of the garden wasn't as obvious as it would have been in one of the nearby town-houses.

Elaine opened the broken garden gate. As she did so, she sighed as she noticed again how much there was to be done. It was even worse now that the warm summer weather had encouraged everything from weeds and grass to privets to grow in great abundance. But there were other priorities.

'Hello, mum. I'm home,' shouted Elaine from the front door.

'Hello dear,' replied her mother from the kitchen. 'You're late home tonight.'

Elaine hadn't thought of an adequate excuse. She couldn't say that she had wanted to avoid the other children, so she answered lamely, 'I decided to walk; it's a nice day.'

Without hardly a pause for breath, she immediately changed the subject before her mother could think too deeply about it. 'What shall we do for tea tonight? There's sausages and beans, or fish-fingers in the freezer,' she added opening the fridge-freezer doors.

Mrs Benistone's face looked anxious. 'Elaine, you work far too hard for a girl of your age; you need to play more. You never bring any of your friends home from school.'

'But you need me, Mum,' argued Elaine insistently. 'Where would you be if I spent all my time messing about and being rude like that awful Michael Jones at school?'

Her mother didn't have the heart to argue. She knew what a help her daughter had been to her. Few people of Elaine's age would respond to the needs of home as she had done.

Mrs Benistone watched gratefully, yet sadly, as Elaine began to pour the oil into the frying-pan.

* * *

The gang were holding their court in the gym cloakroom. The accused was outside munching his chocolate bar, awaiting the results of the proceedings. Andy was presenting evidence to the rest of the gang.

He explained how they'd both got into trouble over the gerbil but it had been all Michael's fault.

'Well,' said Netsie, 'you could have stopped him. You were partly to blame really.'

'You didn't exactly try very hard to stop him,' Claire added. 'How could you just stand there and watch?'

Andy shrugged his shoulders. He had no answer. He didn't know how it happened, either.

'The point is, what are we going to do about him?' asked Mark.

'I think we should kick him out of the gang,' said Emma, who by now had a very clear impression of Michael. 'He's getting worse. And everyone knows he's one of us.'

Andy wasn't against the idea. He agreed that without Michael around, things would be a lot easier.

But Netsie was a moderating influence. 'I don't know really. He's not beyond hope — is he?'

One view of the accused outside munching his chocolate bar might have pursuaded the gang that he was indeed beyond hope.

'We could give him one more chance,' suggested Mark. 'But he's got to stop picking on Elaine and getting us in trouble.'

Emma wasn't giving ground easily. 'If he says one more thing to Elaine, that's it. She'll never want to join us if he goes on the way he's been.'

'Perhaps that's why she doesn't want to come out with us at the weekends or after school,' said Claire. 'She might be so cheesed off with Michael.'

'I think there's more to it than that,' said Mark. 'We'll find out tomorrow after school. Andy, go and tell Michael he can come in now.'

Andy left to fetch the accused for the verdict.

Netsie wanted to be sure that Michael took the whole thing seriously, so she suggested they all stand in a semicircle and not smile. They put a chair in front of them for Michael to sit on.

He was marched in and told to sit in the chair.

Mark began sombrely, 'Some of us felt that you should leave the gang, Michael.' The accused's face dropped. He knew it was coming. 'But after a lot of discussion we've decided to give you one more chance.'

Michael's face lit up immediately.

Emma noticed it. 'This'll be your last chance,' she warned in a voice that reminded Michael of his mum.

Mark continued very officially, 'The reputation of the gang is at stake. You're a year younger than the rest of us. Remember that.'

But Michael saw the ray of hope. 'I'll really try to be better,' he enthused. 'Just give me a week and you'll see a big difference.'

Hopeful, but not totally convinced, the gang let the matter drop. Netsie suggested they next meet on the bus after school.

4

During the next day, the gang kept a close watch on Elaine, looking for the slightest clue that would explain her strange behaviour.

Surprisingly, the girls found her pleasant and friendly. She joined in with the others at break-times, laughing and joking.

It was only when the final bell went that her face began to change — she looked more serious and kept to herself.

On the bus home that Friday night she was sitting all alone gazing wistfully out of the window.

The gang, who usually filled the long back seat of the bus, were letting their curiosity get the better of them. They determined once and for all to discover the mystery surrounding Elaine.

'OK, detectives,' Mark said decisively in a half-attempted American accent, 'this calls for some careful tracking. Netsie, Claire and I will follow close behind her. The rest of you keep back, but follow at a distance.'

It seemed obvious to the gang that the clue to Elaine's behaviour would be found at her home.

When the bus pulled in at the corner of Stockcroft Road, the gang sat tight and waited until Elaine and the other kids had got off. Mark led the others out of the bus. Everyone was unusually quiet.

Elaine started along the road alone. The gang followed slowly until Elaine turned the corner. They made a quick dash and peered round the corner just in time to see her disappear into Church Lane.

'She's taking the shortcut through the cemetery,' whispered Mark.

The minister stood at the church door watching a solitary girl walk by, followed ten seconds later by six other children crouching almost on their hands and knees and leaning into the hedge. A broad smile filled his face as the carnival proceeded out through the far gate.

Suddenly, Michael tripped over a rock and fell into a bramble-bush in the hedge. A cry of pain broke the silence and Elaine turned round.

Just in time, the gang ducked into the gate of 24 Mill Lane. Unfortunately, this was the home of a noisy little Pekinese dog. It certainly didn't intend to stand by in silence with all those intruders at the front gate.

The gang crouched motionless as the dog sounded the alarm to the whole neighbourhood. By the time the concerned owner appeared, Elaine had gone round the next corner. The gang hurried on in relief, leaving the enraged Pekinese still barking loudly, despite its owner's attempts to pacify it.

As Mark cautiously peeped round the corner of Bramble Hill, he saw Elaine disappear into the garden of Magnolia Cottage.

Mark, Claire and Netsie crept on hands and knees through the overgrown garden, closely followed by the others. They crouched below the kitchen window and cautiously peeped in. Elaine was washing dishes and preparing the table for an evening meal.

'Poor girl,' whispered Mark. 'She's doing all the work.'

'Her mum and dad ought to be shot,' criticised Michael.

'Somebody's coming,' warned Andy as the door between the kitchen and the hall opened.

The gang stayed low, sitting beneath the window with their backs to the wall. Through the open window they heard Elaine talking.

'Hello, Mum. I've laid the table and got everything ready for you.'

'That's a good girl,' they heard her mother reply warmly. 'You're always so helpful, love, but you must go and play sometimes.'

The gang slowly raised their heads to peer through the window again. Nothing could have prepared them for the shock that was to follow.

For the first time, they saw Elaine's mother. She was a pleasant-looking woman with fair hair, slightly greying. She was older than they'd have expected. Her clothes were clean and neat, though hardly fashionable.

But these things paled into insignificance as they noticed that she was sitting in a wheelchair.

Elaine hugged her mother and reassured her: 'You need me, Mum. And anyway, I'd rather help you.'

The gang sank slowly to the ground. For once, even

Michael was speechless.

After what seemed like several minutes, Netsie commented as if to herself, 'She didn't say anything about that.' The others were too busy thinking to answer. 'I wonder why.'

'She was probably too embarrassed,' guessed Emma.

'Poor girl,' said Netsie with genuine concern.

Emma, who by nature was very practical, felt it was time for some positive thinking. 'What can we do?'

Nobody had any instant answers so Mark suggested they talk to Rob at the club meeting that night.

* * *

The clubhouse was something special. It was built on the outskirts of Pound Hill right on the edge of the woods. Originally, it was a scout hut and was constructed in the style of a log cabin, with what appeared to be the trunks of trees.

Inside was a huge fireplace and one room. The wood construction gave a warm, cosy feeling to the place.

The church had bought the clubhouse over a year ago. It was just opposite the church building and was an ideal site for a youth club.

Rob was officially the leader of the youth group. He was a farmer in his late thirties, but was quite unlike the normal image of a country farmer. He was robust and sporty and he looked as if he might have been a champion boxer. The more demanding the activity, the more he enjoyed it.

Rob loved kids — and it showed. He had four himself and yet his home was always open to others. It wasn't unusual for there to be eight or more for a meal. He saw the youth work as his extended family.

The Pound Hill Mob — Rob's name for the gang — had a meeting every Friday evening, when Rob had a special time to be with the gang and talk with them. They also had permission to use the clubhouse themselves at any time, providing they kept it clean and tidy.

The gang arrived together during the evening. Strangely, Rob hadn't yet appeared and the door was still locked. It was unusual for him not to be there well ahead of the kids.

Emma was the first to see him. He was over the road in the grounds of the church, talking to the vicar. The gang crossed the road in crocodile formation.

The vicar spotted them approaching. 'Here comes trouble,' he said loudly to Rob, tongue in cheek.

'Do you want the key to the clubhouse?' Rob asked the gang. He threw the key to Mark without waiting for a response.

The vicar noticed Michael's miserable face and asked what the matter was.

Emma saw this as her opportunity to put Michael in his place. 'Come on, Michael,' she said. 'Own up.'

Michael was glad to get it off his chest. He explained that there'd been a new girl at school. 'And I've been making things a bit difficult for her,' he admitted.

To Emma this was a gross understatement. 'Difficult? He put a gerbil in her lunch-box, that's all!'

Rob tried not to smile. The vicar looked away for a moment.

'And I've been calling her names,' added Michael, determined to get it all out.

'Then we found out her mum's in a wheelchair,' Andy said, 'and Elaine has to do all the housework.'

'It's just that she didn't have a school uniform,' Michael continued, hoping to get some little justification for his actions. There was no sympathy, so he moved into self-pity. 'It made a change from everyone picking on me . . . .'

'If you remember my sermon on Sunday,' the vicar butted in, 'it was about the good Samaritan. The point of the story was that we should love our neighbours as ourselves.'

This didn't make any sense at all to Michael. Where was the logic? 'But Elaine lives miles away,' he pleaded.

Rob grinned once again. 'I think you've missed the point there somewhere, Michael,' he said.

'We're all neighbours really, aren't we?' said Claire, to make the point that she, at least, was listening on Sunday.

The vicar nodded. 'That's right. God loves us, however odd we are — and let's face it, some of us are odder than others! — and he expects us to love others in the same way.'

I understand that,' said Michael, not wanting to appear dim. 'But what can I do to put things right with Elaine?'

'Isn't there anything we can do to help?' asked Mark.

'Why not go and see her mother?' advised Rob.

'It appears from what you've said that she'd really appreciate some help.'

'That's a good idea,' said Netsie enthusiastically. 'We'll go round tomorrow morning. It's Saturday.'

5

Early next morning the gang met at the bandstand in the recreation ground.

They waited over ten minutes for Michael to arrive. Just as they were about to set off without him, a panting Michael shouted from the far entrance, 'Oi, hang on a minute.'

Patiently, they waited for Michael's desperate attempt to run the length of the field.

'Congratulations!' they shouted, clapping him on the back. Together, they made their way along Stockcroft Road, discussing how they should approach Elaine's mum.

Just as they turned into Bramble Hill, they saw Elaine coming out of the cottage with a shopping bag in her hand. They sprang back and ran for a low point in the hedge. They scrambled over it, pulling Michael after them.

Elaine passed by totally unaware of the presence of the gang.

'That was a near one,' sighed Andy.

'Yeah,' said Mark. 'Now we can have a chat with Elaine's mum before Elaine gets back from the shop.'

The kids hesitantly approached the front door of Magnolia Cottage.

Mark was aware of the impression that a bunch of six kids might make on a woman at home alone, especially in a wheelchair. So he suggested, 'Netsie and I'll go in. The rest of you wait over by the gate.'

Mark knocked on the door nervously, but a little louder than he'd meant to.

'Who is it?' a voice asked.

'Friends of Elaine's,' shouted Netsie.

'Oh, come in,' invited the same voice.

Mark turned the old brass handle and they stepped into a dark hallway.

'In here.' The voice came from a side room.

Netsie pushed the door open. There, sitting by the breakfast table, was Mrs Benistone, while around the room were piles of laundry, unwashed dishes and the remains of the morning's breakfast.

'Hello,' began Netsie.

'Hello,' replied Mrs Benistone, still a bit taken by surprise.

'Er . . . . This is Mark,' continued Netsie nervously. 'I'm Netsie.'

'It's nice to meet you.' Elaine's mum smiled warmly. 'Elaine's mentioned you, Netsie. You sit next to her in school, I believe.'

'Yes,' said Netsie, relieved that they'd had such a good reception.

'You've just missed Elaine,' her mum continued, assuming that they'd called to see her. 'She's gone to get some shopping for me.'

'Well, actually it's you we wanted to see,' said Mark, taking the initiative. 'The thing is . . . our gang have invited Elaine home a number of times but she won't come.'

'And she seems afraid for us to come here,' put in Netsie.

'I know,' sighed Mrs Benistone. 'It's not easy for Elaine. She's such a conscientious girl. I tell her to go and play with other children, but there's so much to do here.'

Mark and Netsie had certainly noticed. 'She works so hard,' the woman continued, 'but with the housework, the meals, the garden . . . it never seems to end.'

Suddenly, they were rudely interrupted by a noise in the hallway.

'Don't push, don't push!' someone whispered loudly. This was followed by a scuffle and then Michael fell in through the door, his 200 gm bar of chocolate heading straight for the dog-bowl.

Mrs Benistone looked at the heap on the floor and grinned.

'Is he with you?'

'I'm afraid so,' blushed Netsie.

'How many of you are there?' enquired Elaine's mother.

Claire, Emma and Andy popped their heads around the door, highly embarrassed.

'Anybody else?' she said, trying not to laugh.

The gang shook their heads.

Michael, still the centre of attention, got to his feet and wiped the remaining dog-food from his bar of chocolate.

'Does her dad make her do all this work, then?' he asked bluntly.

'I'm afraid Elaine's father died more than a year ago,' explained Mrs Benistone.

Michael's face went red; the rest of the gang bowed their heads.

'She still hasn't really got over it.'

This was Mark's cue to speak up. 'Well, we were wondering if we could help.'

This took Mrs Benistone completely by surprise.

'Well, I just don't know what to say,' she gasped, which was the truth. 'There's certainly plenty to do.'

* * *

What followed can only be described as a working party. You really have to be desperate to accept help from the Pound Hill Mob. No one would doubt their sincerity and eagerness to help, but . . . .

To begin with, Netsie set to work on the pile of laundry that needed ironing.

Claire began to wash the dishes.

Emma decided to tackle the lawn first, while Michael felt the privets would benefit by a trim from his shears.

Andy was concerned that the flowers were watered after the long dry spell, and Mark started with the vacuum-cleaner.

They put a great deal of energy into their tasks and appeared to enjoy every minute of it.

Mrs Benistone just smiled when Andy sent a spray of water through the kitchen window; and Claire only dropped one plate on the flagstone floor.

Mark would have made a much better start, of course, if he'd fixed the vacuum-hose to the end that sucks and not the one that blows.

Emma just couldn't get the lawnmower to work. She pushed, pulled and kicked it, until Netsie pointed out that it needed to be plugged in.

Returning to her ironing, Netsie found a hole in the sheet exactly the same shape as the iron.

Mark was painting the white walls with emulsion. At the same time, he was reading his *Beano*. The distraction led to his painting the kitchen window completely white!

Michael decided to hang out the wet washing. It all went on the line. But he had an artistic way of hanging clothes — upside down, side on or however else it came. Very creative!

But the joy Mrs Benistone had in watching all this youthful activity outweighed the consequences of the 'little accidents'.

When, some time later, Elaine returned from her shopping, the gang had just about finished. The shock would have been great enough to startle her in any event. But as it was, she was greeted by a faceful of spray from Andy's hose.

'What are you all doing here?' she gasped, wiping her face with her handkerchief. Then, realising how different it all looked, she asked stupidly, 'What's happened?'

Andy, already in a good mood, jumped straight in. 'Well, we saw this spaceship appear in the sky.' Acting out the part with great exaggeration, he clowned, 'and two green Martians got out with hosepipes and . . . .'

'Leave off, Andy,' interrupted the new Michael. And, turning to Elaine, he said, 'We just wanted you to know that we'd like to be friends — and that means if you're too busy to come and play with us, we'll come and work with you.'

'Isn't that great, Elaine?' grinned her mum.

Michael still hadn't finished his speech. 'There's one more thing. I really am sorry for being so mean to you, but I never realised all you had to go through. I know it's not much, but I'd like you to have my last piece of chocolate.'

Elaine received the grubby chunk with polite gratitude, but was unsure what to make of it.

Her mum broke the silence by producing a tray of egg-and-cress sandwiches, which she'd made while the gang had been busy.

As they sat on the grass munching their picnic, Michael beamed. 'You know, it's much more fun being nice to people, especially when they give you sandwiches like these.'

In his excitement Michael squeezed his sandwich a bit too hard and a lump of egg-and-cress deposited itself messily on his lap.

In a united chorus, the gang moaned, 'Oh, Michael! Trust you!'

Trap for a thief

1

It was the weekend of The Visit. Michael was to meet his cousin, Reginald, at the station.

Sometimes people's names give you a clue about their character or personality. This was certainly true of Reginald. He was totally different from Michael.

Reginald went to a public school, spoke 'proper' and had an IQ that went right off the top of the graph.

Despite this, Reg always brought a sense of excitement with him. His natural curiosity led him to create the most incredible inventions.

It was for this reason, above all, that Michael waited with enthusiastic expectation for Reg's train to come in.

At four-thirty precisely, the featureless electric train pulled into Three Bridges station. Reginald stepped down from the coach accompanied by a large suitcase and a big grin.

'Hiya, Reg,' shouted Michael. 'Mum's down at the entrance with her car. I've got all those bits and pieces you wanted me to get. They're in the garage. What're you going to do with them?'

'I'll show you tomorrow,' said Reg, not letting

himself be drawn.

* * *

Strange banging and drilling noises were coming from inside Michael's garage the next morning. Unsuspecting neighbours passing by little knew the mischief that was being devised.

Michael watched curiously as Reginald soldered another wire to the strange device on the workbench in front of him.

It was unlike anything he'd ever seen. The basic shape was a box, 20 cm by 10 cm and about 10 cm high. On one side was a series of switches and knobs. Fixed to the top was a TV aerial pointed along the length of the box.

'What exactly is this contraption supposed to do, Reg?' enquired Michael, unable to contain himself any longer.

'Hang on a minute. Just let me solder the interconnecting positive cable to the amplifying adjuster and I'll demonstrate.'

He was giving nothing away until it was completed. Michael was as mystified by the words as he'd been by all the soldering and maze of wires.

Finally, Reg took a set of headphones and plugged them into the appropriate socket on the box.

'There!' he exclaimed with satisfaction. 'Now this gadget works just like a telescope, only with the ears and not the eyes.'

'I see,' responded Michael, none the wiser.

'No you don't; you hear,' quipped Reg to Michael, who missed the joke completely, preferring the

security of his chocolate bar as he bit off a fresh chunk.

'Come on,' he urged, anxious to do his first experiment. 'Put that bar of chocolate away and I'll show you.'

The garden at the front of Michael's house was conveniently screened from the road by a line of privet bushes. The two boys were just tall enough to see over them. It was a quiet cul-de-sac with little or no traffic and it appeared at first glance to be deserted.

Suddenly, Reg spotted them. 'Hey, see those two old ladies over there talking?' Sure enough, about thirty metres down the road on the other side were two women chatting over a garden gate. 'Put the headset on and point the aerial in their direction.'

Michael obeyed.

Reg began to flick switches and turn knobs. The gadget emitted a high intermittent note through the headphones which made Michael jump. He shook his head vigorously.

Then a stupefied look came over his face as he began to hear the voices of the women, as if a radio was being turned up.

'. . . but I never vote myself. Complete waste of time,' he heard the first woman say. 'We only had an election twelve months ago. Why is our mayor resigning already?'

'They say he's emigrating to South America,' came the reply. 'Fine thing for a mayor.'

'Perhaps he knows something we don't.' It was the first woman's voice again.

'I never did like the man. You can tell what someone is really like by his eyes.'

'That's probably why he wears dark glasses!'

Both ladies laughed loudly, catching Michael's ears by surprise and he quickly took off the headset.

Michael was impressed. 'Wow! That's amazing. This'll be great fun. Think of all the secrets we could find out!' Reginald smiled smugly. 'Come on, Reg. Let's show the gang.'

Picking up the gadget, Reginald tucked it under his arm and the two boys set off down the street in the direction of the recreation ground.

The blast of an electronic horn startled their thoughts as Mark Wilson drove right between them on his BMX bike.

'See you at the rec,' he shouted back over his shoulder, narrowly missing a milk-float braking in front of him.

At the field, Mark found the rest of the gang casually standing on the roundabout. Everyone was there, including Elaine. She was sitting on a nearby park bench.

All eyes were on Michael and his cousin as they came on the field at the far end. Everyone was particularly intrigued by what Reg was carrying — a TV aerial on a box, but no TV!

'Here comes Michael,' announced Mark unnecessarily. Elaine came across to see the new arrivals. 'Hey, Michael. What kept you?' Mark added sarcastically.

'Who's your friend with the funny ears?' quipped Andy, observing that Reginald was wearing the headset. Reg took them off promptly.

'Don't you remember I told you about Reg, my cousin from Winchester?' Michael reminded them.

'Oh yes,' twigged Netsie. 'Isn't he the whizz kid? The one with all the weird ideas?'

'Yes. Like the lawnmower that went backwards,' piped up Emma.

'And the remote control plane that didn't fly,' added Claire.

Michael's face reddened noticeably. However, he was still in confident mood. 'But this time it's a great idea!'

'Let's see it then,' demanded Andy, the sceptic.

Everyone gathered round Reg, uncertain whether they were going to have a good laugh over another flop or whether Michael's confidence was really justified.

Reg settled into the role he knew best — impressing

the ignorant. 'All right. Now you see that baby in the pushchair over there?' Nods from everyone. 'It must be two hundred metres away. Right?'

'Right,' responded Claire automatically, clearly unimpressed by this brilliant piece of mathematical deduction. 'So what?'

'Now. Put this headset over your ears and listen,' he ordered authoritatively and proceeded to flick switches and turn knobs.

All eyes were on the mother pushing the baby at the far end of the field. Suddenly, Claire screamed. The baby's piercing cry had almost burst her eardrums.

'Hey, that's amazing!' she exclaimed, giving the invention her seal of approval. 'I could hear the baby's cry right up close, as if it were bellowing in my ears.'

No more scepticism and disbelief; suddenly excitement rose in the gang as all their imaginations were fired at once.

Even Elaine, shy as she was, asked to have a listen to the baby.

Michael's brain was working nineteen to the dozen. The gang liked Reg. More accurately, they liked his invention. This was his chance to take some of the credit. After all, he was the one who introduced Reg to the gang. He ought to be in charge of the gadget.

He discreetly took it from Claire and put it in under his arm, then boldly announced his plan. 'I thought we could go round the town listening in on people's conversations.'

He grinned, anticipating an enthusiastic response. Little did he expect what was to follow.

2

'Are you really sure it's a good idea listening to other people's conversations?' asked Elaine. 'After all, it's a bit different from listening to crying babies.'

Mark's conscience wasn't so troubled. 'Seems all right to me,' he enthused. 'Come on. Let's try it out.'

Netsie was also struggling with the idea. 'It just doesn't seem right,' she sighed, obviously worried.

Michael couldn't stand any more of these damp squibs. It'd be just like the girls to spoil a good idea. Diplomacy was needed. The girls were always good at winning arguments, especially when it came to doing what was right or wrong.

In his most convincing voice he pleaded, 'But we're not doing anything wrong, Netsie.'

Netsie still looked unconvinced.

'It'll be fun,' he added with a grin.

'I think Netsie's right,' confirmed Claire, lending her support to the argument. 'I reckon my mum'd be cross if she found out.'

In a flash, Michael saw his opportunity. Claire had given him the very argument he needed. 'That's the whole point of this invention,' he emphasised. 'Nobody'll ever know.'

The argument sounded convincing. Or maybe the temptation was just too great. Without great conviction, the gang set off across the field.

Mark was determined to bring some light relief to the proceedings.

'I've got a good one,' he said, meaning that he was about to deliver his latest joke. 'How many elephants can you get in a Mini car?'

There was a deafening silence from the gang.

'Two in the front; two in the back,' came the brilliant reply.

'That's pathetic.' Emma was clearly unimpressed.

There was more. 'How many giraffes can you get in a Mini car?' continued Mark, thinking this at least must arouse their curiosity.

'We don't want to know,' replied Netsie, hoping that would be the end of it.

Not likely. Mark wasn't to be put off so easily. 'None.'

Michael looked curiously at Mark.

'There's already four elephants inside!' Mark laughed. The gang groaned, kicking themselves for being sucked into that one.

Andy was about to get in on the act when he noticed two girls from his class heading for the swings at the other end of the field.

His eyes lit up. 'Hey. There's Susan and Jill. I've always wondered what girls talk about?'

Claire sneered. 'Who's kidding who? We all know

Susan's your girlfriend.'

Andy blushed visibly. 'We're just good friends, that's all,' he defended himself unconvincingly. But he didn't intend to lose this opportunity. He turned to Michael and grabbed the gadget. 'Come on, give me the thingummy.'

Andy put on the headset and pointed the aerial towards the girls, who were now sitting on the swings. Reg twiddled the knobs as before.

Andy began to hear a voice. It was Jill's.

'I don't know what you see in Andy Carman, Sue.'

Andy listened with bated breath for the reply. 'Him? Oh, he's wet. He's so daft that he'll get me whatever I ask for.'

Andy's face dropped but he decided to listen to some more. After all, it might get better.

He didn't have to wait long. 'What do you say to him?' Jill asked.

'Andy, if you really liked me you'd bring me a Mars bar tomorrow,' came the reply.

'And does he?' the first voice asked.

'Yes,' continued Susan. 'So far this week I've had one Mars bar, one bottle of Coke and two bags of crisps . . . .'

Andy couldn't take anymore. He removed the headset sheepishly.

Everyone waited expectantly. 'Well?' asked Mark when no response came. 'What were they saying?'

'Er . . . .' Andy began to think fast. 'It's difficult to hear with the noise of the traffic.'

'What traffic?' asked Mark, not believing such a feeble excuse. 'Give it to me.'

Andy gladly handed over the gadget.

'We're not silly, Andy,' pointed out Emma, giving the last word on the subject. 'We know just what Susan thinks of you.'

Michael was anxious not to let this episode spoil their potential for more fun. 'Come on,' he said, leading them out of the field. 'Let's find someone else.'

Mark had another joke. A better one. Everyone braced themselves.

'What's green, has wheels and grows in fields?'

This one sounded more interesting. The gang walked in deep, thoughtful silence but in the end nobody could think of the answer.

'Grass,' Mark announced triumphantly.

'Grass?' asked Netsie incredulously, echoing the thoughts of the others.

'I lied about the wheels,' grinned Mark.

'He's getting worse,' said Emma, confirming what the others were thinking.

The gang reached the shops. Not much opportunity here. They were conspicuous to say the least; the gadget brought many curious stares.

They stopped at the newsagent's for some sweets. Michael pointed out the poster on the news-stand:

'Local Mayor Resigns'.

'That must have been what those women were talking about,' he remarked to Reg.

Chewing to their hearts' content, the gang shuffled on towards the school. In the school-yard there were two teachers in deep discussion, each carrying a pile of exercise books.

Mark spotted them first. He made a grab for the

gadget.

'Quick!' he shouted. 'That's my teacher talking to the headmaster. That'll be interesting. I bet the headmaster's telling him off for not keeping proper discipline in class.'

Emma wasn't impressed with Mark's idea of democracy. She pulled at the aerial. 'Come on, Mark. I haven't had a go yet.'

But Mark wasn't going to let this chance pass.

He pulled it out of Emma's hand. 'No you don't; it's my turn next.'

As Mark slipped on the headset, Reginald had already tuned it in and turned up the volume. Straightaway, Mark heard his teacher's voice.

Imagine his surprise when, in the first sentence he heard his own name mentioned. 'Do you think I'm right in my assessment of Mark Wilson?'

The headmaster replied, 'Yes. Yes, I quite agree. That's what I've always thought.'

Mark pricked up his ears.

'On the surface, he's got the ability to be a good natural leader. But he's so silly. He wastes half his days behaving like a five-year-old.'

This last comment hit Mark right between the eyes. Even the gang had become fed up with his jokes.

'It can't be allowed to continue.' The headmaster was sounding stern.

'Do you think we should contact his father?'

This was going from bad to worse.

'Let's give him another week and see if things improve.'

Mark took off the headset, staring vacantly in front of him, unaware of Emma shouting in his ear.

'Well, Mark, are you going to tell us?'

'I think Mark's just heard some bad news,' announced Michael, with obvious relish.

'Let's go back to the clubhouse,' suggested Mark soberly. 'It's nearly time for the meeting.'

In the far distance, Emma's mum was walking down the road, pushing Elaine's mum in her wheelchair. Emma's mother had visited her several times since Emma told her of the problems she'd been having. They were on their weekly visit to the mini-market.

Emma saw her opportunity. Nobody was going to stop her using the gadget now.

'Oh, look,' she cried, 'There's my mum. Let's have

a quick listen.'

The headset on, her face became knotted in intense concentration. The two mums were some distance away, but she soon caught the gist of the conversation.

It was her mum speaking. 'Well, I envy you, Jean. Your Elaine is such a good girl. I wish Emma would make her bed in the mornings. As for helping with the dishes, she used to be very good. But just lately . . . .'

That was enough. With a sigh, Emma handed back the contraption.

'Here, Reg. You have it. Seems to me that anyone using this machine ends up feeling miserable.' Her face proved the point.

As far as Netsie was concerned, this only confirmed the point she originally made. 'I told you it wasn't a good idea.'

The gang, feeling downcast, began to move off in the direction of the clubhouse. It was more like a funeral procession. No more jokes. No more looking for opportunities to use the gadget.

'Reg always comes up with things that don't work, or things that do work but it'd be better if they didn't,' stated Claire philosophically.

'Whose idea was this in the first place?' asked Mark, looking for a scapegoat.

'I'll give you one guess,' said Emma as all eyes turned to Michael.

Quite oblivious, the culprit was quietly nibbling his chocolate bar.

3

Rob was already at the clubhouse, setting up the dartboard ready for the arrival of the gang.

His greeting was cheerful enough. But the response was almost non-existent. 'So this is your cousin Reggie, is it, Michael?'

Just a nod from Michael.

It didn't take great perception to realise that something was up. 'Well, gang, what's the bad news? You look how I felt the day Brighton lost in the Cup Final!'

Not a grin from anyone.

'Let's talk about it,' Rob said sympathetically. 'It can't be that bad.'

They all sat around on barrels, tables or stools.

'Reg has come up with a new invention,' began Andy, placing the evidence before Rob, who was obviously intrigued by such an original design.

'We've been using it to listen in on other people's conversations,' explained Mark.

'And we wish we hadn't,' confessed Emma,

'because everything we heard made us feel worse than if we'd never known.'

'Knowing everything isn't always such a good idea, is it?' consoled Rob. He thought quickly. 'You know, it's interesting that God made us so that we can tell right from wrong. The Bible says that even people who've never heard of God have a conscience.'

'I told them it was wrong.' Netsie made her point again.

Elaine's deduction was that it was a bad invention.

'Not necessarily,' put in Rob. 'Who remembers, in the garden of Eden, what command God gave Adam and Eve?'

Michael smirked. 'Not to eat any apples.'

Rob couldn't help grinning. 'Actually, there's nothing about apples in Genesis.'

Emma piped up without prompting. 'They were told not to eat any of the fruit from one of the trees.'

'Yes,' said Rob, 'it was the tree of the knowledge of good and evil.'

Andy wondered what all this had to do with their invention.

'Well, one thing we can learn from the story is that God knows best,' Rob explained. 'Adam and Eve would have been all right if they'd listened to what God said.'

But Rob knew he had to bring the whole thing up to date. 'How do you think God speaks to us today?'

Andy came back with the standard answer he'd picked up after many years in Sunday school. 'Through the Bible.'

'Well,' Rob began, wondering how to put it. 'How about the many everyday decisions we have to make? Do we have to keep looking up Bible verses?'

'You mean God speaks to us through the Holy Spirit, when we pray?' asked Mark.

'That's exactly what I mean,' said Rob, pressing home the point. 'You see, when Netsie and Elaine felt uneasy about what was happening, God was speaking to them — through their consciences.'

Mark remembered what he'd heard from his teacher and the headmaster; his lips tightened.

'I'm sure you all realised it was wrong afterwards,' said Rob.

'I think we've learned our lesson this time,' Mark confessed.

Rob sensed it was time to change the subject. He stood up, the darts still in his hand.

'Right. I seem to remember that last week the girls beat the boys at darts. Are you going to let them beat you again tonight?'

The ice was broken amidst vociferous protests from the boys.

* * *

Michael and Reg munched their cornflakes as they watched breakfast TV. The events of the previous day hadn't dampened their spirits and they were looking forward to another day together.

The cartoon finished and they were about to clear away their dishes when they were distracted by a news report. The commentator was interviewing the local mayor. She asked him why he'd just resigned.

'Well, as you know,' the mayor explained in the voice of a politician, 'I was elected last year to serve the good people of Pound Hill and Balcombe. But due to a deterioration in my health, I've been forced to take a complete rest.'

It was hardly exciting stuff. 'Let's go down to the park,' suggested Michael. Reg agreed and went to pick up the gadget.

'Why are you taking that with you today?' Michael asked.

'I just want to test the high frequency response by listening to birds,' explained Reg.

It was quiet at the park that early in the day and the boys crouched down in a corner of the park under a bush, where they wouldn't disturb the birds.

Suddenly, they noticed two men walking along the distant path. One was a plump, middle-aged man, dressed in a pin-striped suit and carrying a brief-case in his right hand.

The other was a younger man with punk-style hair and a large, bent nose. He was dressed in Doc Marten boots, jeans and a bomber jacket.

They were both walking briskly, though the younger man had a peculiar lop-sided gait.

'I recognise that man,' Michael whispered. 'He was on TV this morning.'

'Which one?' asked Reginald.

'You know,' he replied, 'the older one. It's the mayor who's resigning. That one the woman said was going off to South America.'

'Who's he talking to?' Reg wondered.

Michael didn't know either. But one thing he was sure about — they both looked very suspicious.

The men headed off out of the park and into Pound Hill Woods. The boys decided to follow them at a distance. They trailed them for a while, trying not to lose them as the trees became more dense.

Eventually, the men came to a halt and stooped down together. They appeared to be arguing furiously.

The boys hid behind a large fallen tree, trying to catch what was being said. It was frustrating because they were just out of hearing range.

Michael suggested they put the gadget into operation. But Reg wasn't sure after what had happened the previous day and what Rob had said.

'Well,' thought Michael out loud, 'Rob said if we pray about these things we can know if they're right.'

'You pray then,' said Reg, not wanting to take the responsibility for this one.

So Michael screwed his eyes up into what can only be described as a prayerful pose. Reg waited patiently for some kind of response.

Michael beamed. 'Right. I'm sure it's OK this time. After all, they're obviously up to something. Pass me the gadget.'

Reg passed him the headphones and began adjusting the volume. 'It's a long way. I'll open the focus right out and increase the volume to maximum.'

Michael nodded to acknowledge that he could hear. Reg put his ear close to one of the phones so he could hear as well.

'Now listen.' It was the mayor, obviously in a bad mood from the tone of his voice. 'I want no mistakes. We hide the brief-case under these leaves and pick it up in three days, at twelve noon, when the election is over.'

'Yeah. But what if somebody finds it, guv?' whined the punk.

'You idiot,' the mayor shouted at him. 'Who's going to go around cleaning up leaves in the middle of Pound Hill Woods for the next two days?'

He drew close to the punk and lowered his voice. 'Now stay indoors until Friday. And don't come here for any reason.'

The punk nodded stupidly.

With that, the mayor marched off without looking back. The punk thought for a moment, bent down, hesitated, looked towards the mayor and finally sauntered away in a different direction.

Michael took off the headphones and the two boys stood up. 'What a creep! Let's go and have a look at the case.'

Michael led the way as they scrambled over to where the men had been standing, pushing their way through the tall ferns. They arrived at what they assumed to be the spot, but saw nothing.

Reg bent down where there was a large pile of dead leaves. 'Let's try around here,' he suggested.

They ran their hands through the dead leaves. Suddenly, Michael's hand felt something hard and smooth. He rapidly cleared the leaves from that spot to expose the brief-case they'd seen the mayor carrying.

'Come on. Open it, then,' urged Reg impatiently.

But however much Michael pushed, pulled or wiggled the catch, it wouldn't budge.

This was the time for Reg to come into his own. 'Stand back,' he said in his teacher's voice again. 'Leave it to me.'

Reg took another gadget out of the inside pocket of his jacket. This was something Michael hadn't seen before. Could it be another of Reg's weird inventions?

'This is my multi-lock decipher,' came the explanation. 'It opens anything.'

It looked more like the handset of a remote control television, but with a key attachment.

Reg placed the gadget key in the first lock and pressed three buttons. In a flash, the lock sprang open. Michael was amazed. Reg proceeded to the second lock, which opened in the same way.

When Reg lifted open the lid of the case, they weren't prepared for what they saw: £10 notes. The case was packed full of them!

Wrapped in elastic bands and neatly stacked, they looked just like Monopoly money. Only this was no game; it was for real.

Michael was speechless.

'There must be millions there!' commented Reginald. He noticed that Michael was lost in a dream. 'Michael?'

There was no reply.

'Michael!'

Still no reply.

'We've got to tell the police.' Reg knew they had to do something now. There was no way they could ignore this.

Michael came back to earth. He didn't want to give up this adventure so quickly.

'Let's call a gang meeting first,' he suggested. 'Close the case and we'll cover it up again.'

4

Michael was in his element. He was seated on a table in the middle of the clubhouse with the rest of the gang around him on chairs, and Reginald standing to his right side.

Michael could always tell a good tale, and this really was a good one. The gang were lapping it up.

'And when we opened it,' he said, reaching the climax of the story, 'it was stacked full of £10 notes, millions of them!'

'What did you do with the brief-case?' asked Netsie, hoping Michael would suddenly produce all this money.

'We left it where we found it.'

Netsie looked disappointed.

'We couldn't very well take it home. Imagine if Dad found it!' Michael made a credible impression of his father: "Where'd you get all this money, son?" "Oh, I found it, Dad, but the lost property office was closed."'

Everyone grinned. But Netsie was more cautious.

'I think we should tell the police,' she warned.

Michael didn't intend to give up so easily. 'No,' he said. 'Look at it this way. We've got no proof. The mayor would just deny he knew anything about it. Then we'd have some explaining to do. In the end, *we'd* probably be accused of being involved.'

The gang pondered this dilemma.

Mark spoke up. 'Michael's right. Before we go to the police we've got to have absolute proof that the mayor is involved — and where he got the money from.'

Andy had been thinking. 'I've got an idea,' he said.

Nobody heard him, and Emma continued talking to Mark. 'But how can we do that? In two days he'll be gone, and the money, too.'

'I've got an idea,' Andy declared again, still planning it in his mind.

'We really must think of something,' Claire insisted.

By now Andy was so excited about his idea that he was ready to grab their attention.

'Listen. My dad's got one of those video cameras. What if we . . . .' And he proceeded to explain his plan to the rest of the gang.

* * *

The following morning the mayor was at his desk early. It was one day before the election. Not that it would affect him, but he was eager to tie up all his escape arrangements before getting involved in the busy programme of the day.

He was on the phone arguing angrily with his accomplice at the other end. 'I'm paying you enough money as it is. You just make sure I get to Gatwick Airport by four o'clock with my share of the money.'

He was drawing breath to continue, when his secretary unexpectedly walked in. He quickly changed his tone.

'Yes, Mrs Brown, I'll do my very best to ensure that your father gets a hospital bed.'

He paused, pretending to listen to a reply on the phone.

'That's very kind of you, Mrs Brown.'

He smiled hypocritically at his secretary. 'Don't mention it . . . . Thank you. Goodbye.'

He put the phone down firmly and sat back in his chair.

'It's good to know that some people appreciate the hard work I do,' he said to his secretary. 'Now, what's in the post today?'

'Not a lot, sir,' she replied. 'Mostly financial business.'

After showing him most of the post, she produced a large brown envelope. 'Have a look at this one.'

The envelope was boldly marked in Biro along the top:

'*Personal and very private — Dont anybody else open*'.

They both enjoyed the joke together. 'How fascinating,' he grinned. 'I can't wait to open it.'

He slit the envelope with his letter-knife and took out a sheet of lined A4 paper. As he began to read out loud, his face dropped.

Quickly changing the subject, he spoke harshly to

his secretary. 'That will be all, Miss Brokenshire,' he said. 'I'm rather busy at the moment.'

Miss Brokenshire raised her eyebrows, surprised at the sharp change in tone, and left the room.

The mayor watched the door close firmly before reading the rest of the letter. Again, it was written in Biro:

> *'Dear mr Mare, You have been discuvered. We know about your secret atachy case in the woods. If you want your money youd better be there at 3 pm sharpe.*
>
> *The Pound Hill Mob'*

He screwed up the paper and threw it into the wastepaper-basket in a fit of temper.

'Damn!' he yelled, louder than he'd intended.

Miss Brokenshire came running in, alarmed at the outburst. He was taken aback by her sudden appearance.

'Miss Brokenshire, cancel my appointments for the rest of the morning. I'll be out of the office.'

'But, sir, you know that . . .' she began.

'Just do as I say!' he growled angrily, slamming the door as he stormed out, leaving his secretary totally bewildered.

* * *

Deep in the heart of Pound Hill Woods, a great undercover operation was in progress.

Andy was standing in a ditch holding a home video camera and peering over the top of the dense ferns. The rest of the gang were close by, hidden behind a large oak-tree.

Michael was walking towards the spot where the mayor and punk had previously been seen. He was carrying a microphone which was attached by a lead to the video camera and recorder.

He put the microphone carefully down near the brief-case and hid it under some leaves. Moving back towards the others, he gradually buried the complete length of lead under dead leaves so there would be no trace of their presence.

The kids were about thirty metres away from the scene.

'Go and speak to me from where the brief-case is, Michael,' said Andy.

Michael strode back to the case. 'Testing. One, two, three.'

'That's fine,' Andy shouted.

Just as Michael was about to return, he noticed two figures stalking through the ferns. He had to get back to the gang quickly.

Too late. He'd never make it now. He spotted a ditch halfway between the two and made a dive for it. He did a belly-flop into the thick of the ferns and then lay low.

Meanwhile, the rest of the gang saw them approaching and got into hiding. Andy put in the VHS videotape and switched on the recorder. He knelt in the ferns, with the camera pointing over the top.

Fortunately, the camera had a zoom lens so he was able to get a fairly good close-up of the two characters. The microphone was working beautifully and he was able to hear everything through his headphones.

It was the punk. 'I don't like this. What if they've told the police?'

'Be quiet!' The mayor's voice was impatient and commanding. 'Look for the case.'

The punk rummaged through the leaves and was delighted to produce the case. 'It's still here, guv,' he said, relieved.

The mayor wasn't so impressed.

Looking nervously around, the punk added, 'Are you sure this isn't a trap?'

'Just shut up and open it,' the mayor barked.

Fumbling nervously, the punk knelt down, twisted the key in the locks and flicked the case open. The money was all there but to his horror there was a sheet of paper across the top of the money with some words written in bold black felt-tip.

He read it aloud with some difficulty:

'The punk told us'

The mayor took off his glove, leaned over and slapped the punk firmly over his head.

'Ow!' he squealed.

'You idiot!' the mayor exclaimed. 'I told you to keep your mouth shut and stay at home!'

The punk stood up and stammered, 'Honest, guv, I ain't seen nobody. I've spoke to nobody since we done that bank job in South Croydon. This is a set-up.'

'Keep your voice down, you dimwit,' the mayor hissed through clenched teeth. 'You've been a mistake all along. Here's your cut.'

He took a bundle of notes from the brief-case and pressed it into the punk's hand.

'Now get lost. And stay in hiding until I get on the plane tomorrow.'

The punk wandered off, counting his notes as he went.

Behind the tree, Andy gave the thumbs up.

'As good as a confession,' whispered Emma.

But just as they thought everything was in the can, the punk tripped over Michael lying in the ditch. He regained his balance just in time to stop himself falling right on top of Michael.

'Oi, guv, there's a kid!' he shouted back.

Michael sprang to his feet in total surprise.

The mayor bellowed, 'I can see it's a kid, you fool.'

'But . . .' the punk muttered.

'Well, don't just stand there. Go get him.'

'Oh! Yeah!' The punk reached out for Michael, who ducked and made a dash for the tree.

'Hey, you lot, I need help!' Michael pleaded.

Suddenly, out from behind the tree sprang six

more kids, including Andy with a video camera in one hand and a VHS tape in the other.

The punk was totally baffled. 'Oh, heck, guv, there's a whole load of 'em now!'

The mayor was infuriated. 'I can see that, you idiot.'

'Oh.' The punk acted stupid.

'Well, go get them, then!'

'What? All of them?' The punk looked from one to the other.

Then the mayor noticed Andy. 'Get that videotape before they get away.'

'Right, guv,' the punk replied as he tried to grab Andy. The gang ran for it.

The mayor dropped his case and joined in the pursuit. When the punk grabbed Andy by the shoulder, he instinctively called to Mark, 'Catch!'

Mark turned, holding out his hands. He grabbed the tape Rugby-fashion and bolted – straight into the arms of the mayor.

The mayor should have grabbed the tape, but instead grabbed Mark, who threw the tape to Claire. She fumbled and dropped it.

The punk made a dive for the tape but Andy was there first. The mayor and the punk converged on him together.

In desperation, Andy threw it high in the air, where it seemed to linger in suspended animation until it came straight down into the hands of – the mayor.

He gloated over his acquisition. 'Ha, the Pound Hill Mob!' he grinned, surveying them in turn. 'Nothing more than a bunch of stupid kids.'

'Yeah, stupid kids,' echoed the punk.

'You're lucky I don't have time to deal with you

properly,' he continued menacingly.

'Yeah, properly,' came an imitated echo from the punk.

'But seeing as I now have the videotape, you've got no evidence. So, get lost,' barked the mayor.

'Yeah, get lost,' sneered the punk.

Emma wasn't to be so easily intimidated. 'You won't get away with this,' she threatened.

'Nothing can stop me now,' said the mayor, taking Emma's comment with a pinch of salt.

'Nothing can stop him now.' It was the punk again, who was beginning to irritate the mayor with his pathetic parroting.

The mayor turned on the punk angrily, 'Oh, shut up, will you?' And he stalked off, clutching the tape.

The punk, half oblivious, was still enjoying his role as a gangster, thinking he was proving menacing to the kids. He started up again: 'Yeah, shut up will . . . .'

Two things suddenly dawned on him: first, the mayor had gone, and second, why was he telling the children to shut up when they weren't saying anything? In acute embarrassment, he turned on his heels and bolted after the mayor in his usual awkward manner.

The gang stood rooted to the spot, speechless.

'Now what can we do?' asked Elaine eventually, sensing the hopelessness of the situation and the waste of all their good efforts.

'I don't know,' said Mark, who usually had some idea in an emergency. 'He's got the tape — we haven't got any evidence.' That was the cold, brutal logic of their position.

Only Andy didn't seem so downhearted by events. Slowly, he pulled a VHS videotape from inside his jacket.

'Oh yes, we *have* got evidence!' he proclaimed, brandishing the tape before their eyes.

Everyone was amazed. With their own eyes they'd all seen the mayor walk off with the tape.

'He did take *a* tape,' grinned Andy, 'but not *the* tape with the evidence on. I gave him the tape that was in the recorder before we started.'

A sigh of relief swept through the whole gang as they realised they'd got what they'd wanted after all.

'Well,' Mark concluded, grinning from ear to ear, 'let's get down to the cop-shop, then.'

5

Pound Hill police station was a substation manned only during office hours. There were usually two officers, at the most, on duty.

They weren't used to big crime in Pound Hill; stray cats, noisy neighbours and false alarms were the order of the day. So for Sergeant Jackson and Constable Cassidy to be confronted by such a large, vociferous bunch of kids — and with such an incredible tale — was a turn-up for the book.

'Sounds like a tall story to me,' said the constable. 'It'd be far too embarrassing to search the mayor's house without a very good reason.'

'But this video proves it,' said Andy, holding the tape virtually under his nose. 'If only you'd go and play it, you'd see.'

The sergeant agreed to watch the video. After all, it'd be best to play the whole thing down and let them enjoy their little joke. He, too, had been young once.

He ushered the whole gang into the back room

where there was a video recorder and television set.

The constable put the tape into the recorder, rewound it and pressed PLAY. At first there was a blur, followed by some out-of-focus clowning by Michael holding a microphone.

Eventually, the picture settled down. The mayor and the punk appeared on the screen. At times their heads were missing and there was some excessive zooming by the 'cameraman'. But the sound was good. And certainly there was no denying that the kids had been telling the truth.

The sergeant wasn't without a sense of humour.

'I don't think Steven Spielberg has anything to worry about from you lot,' he said, adding more seriously, 'But the mayor obviously does. Constable, take three of the children in your car and I'll take the rest in mine. We'll pay the mayor a visit.'

* * *

The mayor was relieved to have dealt with the kids so easily. He arrived home to collect his air-tickets and make final arrangements.

It would be better for him to be at the airport early, away from Pound Hill. There was no knowing whether the children might start talking to their parents and stirring up trouble.

He double-checked the money in his brief-case. There was no need for him to take anything other than a few clothes and toiletries. After all, he now had enough money to buy anything he wanted for the rest of his life.

He still had the videotape he'd taken from the

gang. He was about to throw it in the bin, as he was leaving the room, when curiosity got the better of him.

Switching on the TV, he put the tape in the recorder. 'I wonder just how much they managed to get?' he mused as he settled down to wait for the picture to appear.

What appeared, however, was Charlie Chaplin being chased down a cliff path by a couple of policemen. The awful truth dawned on him. He'd somehow been tricked. This wasn't the tape.

'Oh, no!' he groaned involuntarily.

'Oh, yes!' came the response. It was Emma. She burst into the room followed by the rest of the gang.

The mayor fumed, 'What are you kids doing here? You've made a big mistake.'

'I'm afraid it's you who's made the mistake, sir,' the sergeant insisted as he followed the gang in. 'Thanks to these kids, you'll soon be behind bars.'

* * *

Several weeks passed. For some days, at least, the gang had been the talk of Pound Hill. Even the local paper had carried a photograph and a feature.

But fame is as short-lived as people's memories. School routine and homework at night soon made ordinary people of the gang again.

The whole incident had almost passed into history when one morning, just before assembly, a large police car pulled into the school-yard and what appeared to be a high-ranking policeman asked directions to the headmaster's study.

Everybody knew that something was up when they were told at registration that assembly would be extended for the whole of the first period.

The hymn was short enough, an old favourite, '*Morning has Broken*'. Mr Hawtin told the school to sit and then beckoned the officer to the stage. He coughed to clear his throat and began.

'Now, school, we are very fortunate to have Chief Inspector Baldwin of the Crawley CID here with us today. No, Jeremy, he hasn't come to arrest me.

'I'm sure you'll remember that, not too long ago, some children from this school were in the news. Will the children from the Pound Hill Church Youth Club please come forward?'

There was a bustle of excitement as the gang made their way to the front. What was this all about? What could have happened?

'I believe you call yourselves "The Pound Hill Mob". Sounds to me more like a bunch of criminals than detectives.'

He paused to allow the mixture of laughing and groaning to subside. 'The inspector has some very interesting news for you.' He turned to the visitor. 'They're all yours.'

The inspector began to waffle, as those who aren't experienced at talking to kids often do. Noticing rather a lot of shuffling from the back of the hall, he made a determined effort to get to the point:

'Well, the bank in South Croydon were so grateful for your help in ensuring the speedy return of their money that they've opened accounts for you at their local branch and have deposited £100 each for you.'

The gang were taken completely off-guard by this

news. Nobody had told them about any reward!

They were still taking it in when the inspector continued. 'As for Reginald, the bank decided to open a business account for him in Winchester. And when he reaches the age of eighteen he'll receive an investment of £500 to help him market his first invention.'

Michael was thinking out loud. 'How many bars of chocolate can I get for £100?'

The inspector heard his calculations and shattered his dreams with one final piece of information.

'Of course, you won't be able to touch the money until you're sixteen.'

The corners of Michael's mouth turned down.

'But it will gain interest.'

Michael looked at Andy. 'Sounds *interest*ing. Get it?'

One of those days

1

It may not have been the most exciting event of the year, but the Women's Institute Jumble Sale was always worth a visit.

If you were quick, you could pick up some good bargains in books and comics. The best ones were often to be had just before closing time, when the old ladies were prepared almost to give away what was left.

Andy needed only one round of the tables and their 'attractions' to see that this wasn't going to be a profitable visit. There'd been too many kids before him with plenty of pocket money to spare.

As Andy stepped out of the musty room into the bright sunshine, he was surprised to see his dad walking down the street. Mr Carman was normally at work at this time of day.

'Hi, Dad,' shouted Andy. 'What are you doing home?'

Taken off guard, Mr Carman mumbled, 'I'm busy at the moment. See you later.'

With a puzzled look on his face, Andy strolled casually along the pavement. A great day lay ahead.

He spotted the girls from the gang leaning over the gate, feeding a contented-looking horse.

Emma saw him first. 'Hello, Andy. Where are you going?'

'Up to Mark's,' he replied, walking by. 'We're going off for the day.'

There was no time to waste talking to the girls. Today was going to be a great day.

Andy's thoughts were rudely interrupted by a clattering noise ahead. Oh, no! It was the punk, and the noise was a beer-can he was kicking along the road.

And who was the fellow with him? He looked even worse than the punk. He must have been over two metres tall!

It was too late to cross the road. It'd look obvious. Andy put his head down and began to speed up his walk.

They were on a collision course. The punks stopped. Andy stopped. Face to face.

Andy thought fast. He stepped to his right and the punk moved out to block him. Andy moved back, then pretended to go to the left. The punk's friend blocked him.

Quick as a flash, Andy dived through the gap between them and bolted up the road.

The punk and his friend turned and grinned. They weren't interested in exerting themselves. Andy gave a sigh of relief, spotted the discarded beer-can and kicked it angrily into the ditch.

It was only a short walk to Mill Lane and Mark's home. Andy turned into the drive, much relieved, and knocked on the door. He turned back to make sure he hadn't been followed.

Mr Wilson opened the door and, recognising the back of his head, said, 'Hello, Andy.'

'Hello,' said Andy, spinning round. 'Is Mark home?'

'No,' replied Mr Wilson. 'He's gone to the dentist for a check-up. He'll be back soon.'

'I think I'll go meet him,' said Andy.

'Oh, Andy,' Mr Wilson said as he saw an opportunity. 'If you're going past the newsagent's, would you get me a *Daily Mail*?'

'Yes, of course,' replied Andy, taking the 50p coin from Mark's dad.

Then he remembered that the punk and his crony were on the loose!

'Er . . . Mr Wilson.'

'Yes.'

'Do you think I could borrow Mark's bike?' He could see Mark's dad hesitating. 'Just to get the paper,' he added as an afterthought.

'I'm sure Mark won't mind,' smiled Mr Wilson.

'Thanks,' grinned Andy, much relieved.

Andy was off to a good start. He now had Mark's new computer-controlled BMX all to himself for a good while.

He skilfully changed into hyperthrust and, coming round the corner to the newsagent's at 150 mph, jammed on his brakes and screeched to a halt amidst the vociferous protests of a noisy little Pekinese dog tied up outside.

'Not that stupid dog again,' he thought.

He leaned his bike against the shop wall and went in.

Typical! There was a queue. Andy decided to

browse through the comics until the queue shortened.

Meanwhile, Mark was returning from the dentist, greatly relieved that he'd been given a clean bill of health. Safe for another six months!

To his amazement, as he approached the newsagent's, he saw his own bike leaning against the wall. Not only that, but a little Pekinese dog was causing potential rust to his chain.

'Hey, someone's pinched my bike,' he said audibly. 'Get off, you pesky dog!' he shouted, jumping on the bike.

He rode home wondering who could have stolen his bike, but relieved to have got it back.

Meanwhile, Andy had the shock of his life when, coming out of the newsagent's, he noticed that the borrowed bike was missing.

'Hey, someone's pinched the bike!' he shouted to no-one in particular.

A well-dressed man in a striped suit, who was coming out of the shop reading his *Times*, was taken aback by a boy shouting in his right ear.

'What happened?' he said.

'The bike's disappeared! I left it here a minute ago. Now it's gone.'

The man stepped out into the road, looking intently to the right and left. Nobody. He shrugged his shoulders and stepped into his Volvo, pausing to finish the front page at the steering-wheel.

The excitement brought the shopkeeper into the street. 'What's up, Jack?' he asked the man in the car.

'Somebody's stolen this kid's bike,' said the man

through the open window. He started the engine and drove slowly off.

'I'll notify the police,' volunteered the shopkeeper to Andy.

Andy was nervous of bringing the police in at this stage, especially as he thought he'd probably get in trouble for leaving the bike unattended for so long.

'Let me go back and tell Mark's dad first; it's Mark's bike.'

In the meantime, Mark had already arrived home. Mr Wilson answered the door to an excitable son.

'Dad, someone stole my bike! I found it outside the newspaper shop.'

'Oh, Mark!' Mr Wilson clasped his forehead.

'What's the matter, Dad?'

'Andy just borrowed your bike to go to the shop for me.'

'Now, how was I to know that?' thought Mark, but said nothing.

Mr Wilson continued, 'You'd better get back to the shop quickly and tell him before he gets worried.'

Mark sprang on to his bike and sped down the drive, shouting over his shoulder, 'I'll go the bottom way; it'll be quicker.'

Mr Wilson doubted the wisdom of this and opened his mouth to reply. Too late. Mark was around the corner and out of sight.

Before he could close the door, he had evidence of his own convictions as Andy came running round the corner.

'Mr Wilson,' shouted Andy, 'someone stole Mark's bike while I was in the shop.'

Mr Wilson sighed. 'No they haven't; it was Mark. Didn't you pass him on the way?'

'No.'

'Which way did you come?'

'Down Victoria Road,' replied Andy, getting more confused.

'Typical,' groaned Mr Wilson, 'Mark went round the bottom way.'

'I'll go and tell him,' said Andy enthusiastically, ready to run off down the road again.

This time Mr Wilson intervened. 'No you don't. I think we'll stay here until everyone is present and correct.'

Oblivious to all this, Mark was on the way to the newsagent's when a car coming in the other direction braked and a man got out carrying a newspaper. He came across the road and waved Mark down.

'Where did you get that bike?' he demanded.

'It's mine,' replied Mark, taken by surprise.

'This looks like the bike that was stolen outside the newsagent's,' the man insisted.

How could Mark explain this one?

'There was a mix-up,' he began. 'My friend borrowed my bike. But I didn't know it. I came by and thought it'd been stolen. So I took it. Then he came out and also thought it'd been stolen. Now I'm looking for him to tell him I've got it.'

The man was dumbfounded. 'Well, that's the best story I've heard today. But your friend left the shop five minutes ago. I should try back at your place.'

Wondering where this would all end, Mark turned and headed back towards home, when who should come cycling straight out from the side road without looking but Michael.

'I thought you'd passed your cycling proficiency test,' Mark shouted as they almost collided.

'My brakes are a bit wonky,' confessed Michael, trying to get the brake-block to bite the wheel.

'Yeah,' retorted Mark, not at all impressed; 'and when you fall off and land on your head, that'll be a bit wonky, too, if you don't get them fixed.'

'What?' said Michael, frowning, not in the least impressed by Mark's logic. Changing the subject, he asked, 'What are you doing today?'

'Well, when I track Andy down,' said Mark, remembering his problems, 'we're going on a long bike ride.'

'Great, can I come?' ventured Michael, not missing an opportunity.

'What! On that bike? You'll never be able to keep up, Michael.'

'I will,' Michael insisted. 'Dad oiled it last week.'

'Are you sure he didn't oil your brake-blocks?' suggested Mark sarcastically.

Michael's puzzled expression confirmed the fact that the joke had been lost on him.

'All right,' Mark conceded. 'But if you get tired you'll have to find your own way back.'

That was good enough for Michael, who was now determined to prove himself. 'I'll race you home, then.'

'On that bike?' queried Mark disbelievingly.

'Well. You'd better give me a ten-start,' decided Michael, just to be safe.

'One, two, three, four, five, six, seven . . . .'

Michael was around the corner and out of sight, so Mark saw no point in counting any further. His right foot went hard down on the pedal and he lowered his head to minimise wind resistance.

Michael put all his might into the race, but Mark was slimmer and, it must be said, fitter. They turned the corner to Mark's house together but on the last stretch Michael finally ran out of steam and reluctantly watched Mark streak ahead.

Leaning his bike against the garden wall, Mark offered his condolences. 'Good try, Michael. Better luck next time.'

The door was answered by Andy. 'Hello Mark. Fancy seeing you. Do come in.' And then to Michael, 'Bit early in the day for you, isn't it, Michael?'

'Now we're all here, let's go get your bike,' Mark suggested to Andy.

Andy jumped on behind Mark and sat on the saddle.

'This morning,' he confided to Mark, 'Dad was acting really strangely again. Just lately he seems to lose his temper so quickly and at home he always thinks I'm creeping up on him all the time.'

Mark was unable to offer any explanation.

* * *

Not far away, in the churchyard, Andy's dad stood looking blankly at a gravestone. Quite oblivious of anyone or anything else, he drew out a half-bottle of brandy from his pocket and began to drink slowly.

* * *

Meanwhile, the punk and his friend, Bonzo, had made their way to Pound Hill Woods. As usual, they were up to no good.

'How did the mayor escape, then?' asked Bonzo.

'I had to hire two powered hang-gliders out of my cut of the money,' moaned the punk.

'Where's he gone?'

'Last time I saw him he was heading west.'

The punk looked casually over his shoulder. 'Once all this has died down he wants to pull off another job to get some more cash. When he's ready, he'll get in touch.'

He sucked the last drop of beer out of his can and issued a challenge. 'Right. Get this one.'

He threw the empty can high into the air. Bonzo picked up a nearby stone and aimed it casually as the can reached its highest point.

'Missed!' proclaimed the punk with glee.

The smile was only wiped from his face by the ping of the can landing on the crown of his head.

2

The boys always enjoyed cycling in the woods. They spent most of their time building imaginary stunt courses.

Just recently, an old oak tree had blown down in a gale and formed a bridge over a marshy gully. With the help of a couple of old planks, they'd been able to construct a ramp.

Mark and Andy set off across the tree with no real problems. Then it was Michael's turn. He remembered Mark's earlier words and wasn't about to be left behind.

He moved forward, eyes firmly fixed on the far branches of the tree. Then his front wheel began to wobble in response to his nervous arms.

There followed two disastrous mistakes. First he looked down. Then he put his right foot down to steady himself, forgetting there was nothing beneath him.

Michael fell gracefully, bike and all, into a large patch of bracken.

'Nice one, Michael!' shouted Andy, racing on.

'Send us a postcard,' added Mark as they disappeared over the crest of a hill.

'Oi, wait for me!' pleaded Michael in vain, as he hauled his bike out of the bracken.

Realising that his request had fallen on deaf ears, he pulled out his latest bar of chocolate and bit off another three squares.

Had Mark and Andy known what was waiting for them around the corner, they might not have been so anxious to hurry on. What they failed to hear was a drunken chorus of *She'll be Coming Round the Mountain*.

They turned the corner at breakneck speed and slammed on the brakes just in time to prevent themselves crashing into the two layabouts.

Bonzo and the punk were delighted at the prospect of some new entertainment. Bonzo grabbed Mark's handlebars from the front.

'You want to watch where you're going. Someone could get hurt.'

'And that someone is standing right in front of me,' added the punk, positioning himself in front of Andy's bike.

Mark was annoyed. 'What are you doing around here again?' he said to the punk. 'I thought . . . .'

'You shut up and mind your own business,' Bonzo interrupted.

The punk drew close to Andy's face and growled deliberately, 'I hate kids who stick their noses into other people's business.'

Bonzo saw the opportunity for some excitement. 'Give me your bike,' he ordered Mark.

'Not likely,' Mark replied boldly. With that, Bonzo

gave him a firm push to the left, causing him to roll on to the ground.

'Come on, Chisel-face,' he shouted at the punk gleefully as he jumped on the bike. 'Take the other one.'

The punk drew Andy's face close to his and put on one of his grimmest expressions. Speaking in almost a whisper, he said, 'If you don't give me the bike, my mate Bonzo here'll pull your nose off.'

So saying, he pushed Andy firmly off the back.

The two layabouts were in their element. Behaving like the children they were, they sped up and down on the bikes, occasionally crashing into each other.

The punk picked up a small branch; now they were knights of old charging with lances.

Mark and Andy looked on in despair. 'What are we going to do?' sighed Andy.

Mark had no answers. 'There's nothing much we can do except wait. Maybe they'll get tired,' he offered with little hope.

Meanwhile, behind them, Michael suddenly appeared around the corner, having disentangled himself and satisfied his hunger. He hadn't expected to catch up with them so quickly.

In a flash, he assessed the situation and dived back behind the wall before anyone noticed him.

What could he do? Even the three of them couldn't take on those two yobs. It was too far back to go and get help. What would scare them off?

Suddenly, an idea came. 'Hey, Mark,' he shouted deliberately loudly. 'There's a couple of coppers down here. Do you want me to go and get them?'

The two villains stopped in their tracks. 'Let's get out of here,' shouted Bonzo. 'You'll see us again,' he growled at the boys as they ran off.

'Not if we see you first,' shouted back Mark, defiantly.

Michael hopped on his bike, beaming from ear to ear.

'That was great, Michael,' complimented Mark.

'Quick thinking, Michael,' chirped in Andy, and as an afterthought, '*Were* there any coppers?'

Michael grinned and put his hand in his pocket. 'There were a couple,' he announced, showing them two copper coins.

For the first time, Andy and Mark were speechless.

Michael was now bubbling over with confidence after the incident. 'Are we going on?' he suggested.

'Not me,' said Mark categorically. 'I don't want my bike smashed up.'

'Nor me.' agreed Andy. 'We might just bump into them again.'

'And I might not be there to save you next time,' put in Michael.

'All right, Superman,' said Mark, feeling that Michael was going a bit too far and would need bringing down a peg or two.

There was nothing like another bike race for that. Michael foolishly offered to race them back to the clubhouse.

But his new-found confidence was from the neck upwards. His body still struggled with his human limitations and he arrived puffing and panting fifty metres behind the other two.

* * *

The girls had been at the clubhouse all morning. They'd decided to go in for a local poster competition and were all busy working with poster-paint on a large sheet of white paper.

It was a great surprise to see the boys back so soon. 'I thought you were all going off for the day,' queried Emma.

'Yeah, well, that's another story,' volunteered Mark,

half-embarrassed. He wasn't keen to be shown up in front of the girls.

Michael, who wasn't nearly so concerned for his reputation, blurted out, 'That punk's back in the area again, and he's got a mate with him.'

'They'd been drinking,' explained Mark, just to convince the girls of what they were up against.

Andy decided it was time to change the subject. 'What are you girls doing?'

The girls explained that Rob had suggested they enter a competition organised by the Pound Hill Tourist Bureau; they had to portray the delights of Pound Hill for holidaymakers.

The big attraction, as Emma was quick to point out, was the prize of £50.

Michael began to think figures. Out came his pocket calculator. Fifty divided by ninety-three makes 0.5376344. This looked interesting.

'Hey,' he shouted for attention, 'do you know that you could get fifty-three and a half bars of chocolate with that?'

'Oh, Michael!' Emma was exasperated. 'Can't you think of anything else?'

Remembering what they'd really come for, Mark asked the girls if Rob was around.

Claire told him that Rob was still on the farm and would be there for the rest of the day.

Poster painting wasn't what the boys had in mind for a Saturday.

'Come on, you two, let's go see him.' The boys left as quickly as they'd come.

As they belted along the road to the farm, Michael puffed and panted. Why did Andy and Mark always have to be trying for a world record everywhere they went?

If they hadn't been in quite such a hurry, they might have noticed Andy's dad, who was walking down a side lane near the farm. His slow, stumbling walk revealed that he had taken more brandy than he could handle.

Finally, unable to maintain his equilibrium, he stumbled and fell into a mucky ditch where he lay in a state of semiconsciousness.

3

At the farm, Rob was busy sawing logs to replenish his store for the autumn.

As he cut the logs, he loaded them on to the trailer hitched to his red Honda trike. This big three-wheeler with the balloon tyres was an ideal machine for getting across the rolling fields. It was capable of coping with most gradients and could reach a speed of 50 mph over some of the most uneven or marshy surfaces.

The loud hum and vibration of the chainsaw took Rob's attention. He was totally unaware of the boys' arrival. The first indication he had was of a voice shouting 'Rob!' close to his left ear.

He switched off the saw. Turning round, he was surprised to see three familiar faces.

'I thought you boys were off cycling for the day.'

'Yes, we were,' admitted Mark.

'We ran into the punk,' added Michael, 'and he's got a new friend called Bonzo — a real hard case.'

Rob smiled to himself. He'd met this Bonzo before.

He wouldn't have called him a 'hard case' — more of a soft-head. Though he was tall and looked fierce in an odd sort of way, he had the mentality of someone half his age.

But, Rob reasoned, Bonzo lived at Handcross, twenty miles away. If he'd teamed up with the punk, they would be up to no good.

Michael broke in again: 'We can't seem to go anywhere without bumping into them.'

'Those two need help, if only they knew it,' advised Rob. 'Of course, being out of work doesn't help.'

Rob remembered the difficult times he'd had before he owned the farm: the six months he'd spent looking for work without success and how, during that period, he and Pam had lost their only child.

He knew what it was like to have a rough deal from life's circumstances. It was through those experiences that he had begun to work with young people. He, if anybody, knew that there was hope, even for the dropouts of society.

'But they need more than a job,' he continued.

'What they need is twelve months in Dartmoor prison, so that we can get on with things,' commented Mark, from a completely different perspective.

'The fact is, Mark, at this stage they need help rather than punishment, before it's too late,' said Rob, trying to correct Mark's perspective a little.

Whatever the rights and wrongs of the argument, the boys were keen to stay on the farm for the rest of the day, and Rob was happy to agree to this.

In fact, he had a surprise for them. 'Jump on the trailer, boys,' he shouted, and they sped off up the rough lane to the farmhouse. The boys clung to the sides, cushioning themselves against potential bruising.

Once in the farmyard, Rob headed straight for the garage. The boys jumped off, rubbing their somewhat tender bottoms.

With a big show, Rob opened the garage door to reveal another Honda three-wheeler, this time a miniature version, just the right size for the boys!

Rob watched with a thrill the delight on their faces as it dawned on them that they were going to spend the afternoon testing it. But he wasn't about to let them loose on a new bike without ensuring that they knew how to handle the machine.

First, he explained the gears and warned them to use only first and second gears until they were more experienced. He demonstrated how to make the trike go faster by squeezing the accelerator trigger.

But most of all, he made sure they each knew how to operate the brake. If all else failed, they had to be able to stop!

It seemed to the boys that, after such a disastrous start to the day, things hadn't turned out so badly after all.

They took it in turns racing the trike up and down the large field. It was an ideal stunt course — a steep bank at one end, a marsh and pool in the corner, a long flat section for speed-racing and an interesting piece of undulation where the field looked like a large sheet of corrugated iron.

* * *

The girls had finished their poster and were keen to

get to the farm themselves. Pam had agreed to have them all round for a real cream-tea. The girls themselves had helped to make the jam from the strawberries they'd picked the previous week.

As they locked the club hut and set off down the lane, they were in high spirits. Pleased with their day's work, they were now looking forward to a fun evening.

'You'll never guess what,' announced Emma.

'What?' said Claire, as if she could have said anything else.

'You know it was my birthday last Tuesday?'

'Oh yes,' said Claire, realising she had totally forgotten. 'Did you get anything good?'

'I had some lovely nail-varnish from Gran,' Emma replied with genuine enthusiasm. 'But my aunty sent me a doll. I think she's forgotten how old I am. I could give it away to someone.'

Claire saw the cue for a song. '*You've got yourself a crying, talking* . . . .'

The other girls caught on, recognising the tune of *Living Doll*: '. . . *sleeping, walking, Sindy doll*!'

Emma soon got into the swing of things. '*I've got to do my best to please her just cause she's my Sindy doll.*'

It was in this state of giggles that the girls suddenly and unexpectedly came across Andy's dad lying in the ditch.

The smiles were wiped from their faces as they gazed in disbelief at the sight of Mr Carman, unshaven, scruffy-looking and as far as they could tell unconscious or maybe even dead.

Their worst fears were dispelled when he groaned and tried to raise his head.

'Mr Carman, are you all right?' asked Emma, deeply concerned.

There was only a faint groan in reply. Netsie took control of the situation. 'Quick, Claire, run and get Rob.'

4

Rob was deep in thought as he unloaded logs from the trailer into the wood-store. Suddenly, he was disturbed by a shrill voice calling out his name. It was Claire.

'Rob, Rob, come quickly! We've found Mr Carman lying in a ditch. He may have hurt himself, and he smells of drink.'

Rob stared in disbelief. It didn't sound like the kind of thing David Carman would do. Still, he ought to go and look anyway — and with Claire pulling on his jumper he had little option.

As they arrived at the scene, David was just beginning to come round. The three girls were bent over, trying to talk to him.

Rob knelt close to his head. 'Are you all right, David?'

There was an almost inaudible groan.

Rob noticed the empty brandy bottle in his hand. 'Oh, no. What's this all about?' Rob threw the bottle disdainfully in the air and over the hedge.

'I've done the wrong thing,' was the pathetic response from Andy's dad.

Stooping, Rob helped him to stand. 'You could do with a mug of strong coffee. Come back to my place.'

He pushed Mr Carman's arm around his own shoulder and helped him stumble along. The girls followed silently, not knowing quite what to make of it all.

* * *

The boys were having the time of their lives on the trike. As they gained confidence, they began to go faster. They discovered that by holding on to the handlebars and leaning back, they could do wheelies riding just on the two back tyres.

Once, Mark began to panic because, although he managed to get the bike to do a wheelie, he couldn't get it down again.

With the front wheel in the air, he couldn't steer the trike. Heading straight for the hedge at 40 mph, he lost all power to control the machine.

In a last desperate effort, he jerked forward and got the front wheel on the ground again. He swerved just in time to miss the hedge.

What he forgot was that, when turning right on a trike, you don't lean to the right as you would on a bike; you lean the opposite way, to the left.

The result was devastating. The bike began to shake, Mark jammed on the brakes and the trike came to a halt, rolling on its side.

Mark escaped unhurt but shaken. But after that, the boys became content with less adventurous escapades.

Unbeknown to the boys, lurking in the woods by the edge of the field were two figures. As they peered over the stone wall at the boys enjoying themselves, one thought went through both minds simultaneously.

The bike came to a halt and Michael was about to hand over to Andy. Suddenly, quite unrehearsed, the two figures dived over the wall and bolted for the trike, pushing the boys out of the way.

Bonzo jumped on the saddle and began to rev up. The punk was still pushing the boys back when the trike moved off.

'Wait,' he shouted angrily. Unfortunately, Bonzo obeyed. 'My foot! My foot!'

'What?' shouted Bonzo, trying to hear him over the noise of the revving of the engine.

'You're on my foot. Get off!'

'Oh.' And the trike edged forward.

The punk started to hop around clutching his painful left foot. Bonzo, thinking it was time to get going, accelerated away.

The punk wasn't going to be left behind with the kids and dived at the bike, grabbing a handle behind the saddle. Clutching as if his life depended on it, he was dragged fifty metres on his belly, shouting and screaming for Bonzo to stop.

There were several angry blows before they agreed together that the punk could sit in the saddle while Bonzo stood and steered.

Now they were really in their element.

* * *

In Rob's kitchen there was a strong, pleasant smell of freshly-filtered coffee. Pam had left the room, leaving Rob and Mr Carman seated together at the old pine dining-table.

Rob said very little at first until he thought David Carman was relaxed and ready to talk. When they had finished their coffee, he asked him what had happened to make him behave the way he had.

'My brother, Jim, died a few months ago,' Mr Carman began hesitantly. 'Jean — my wife — and young Andy seemed to get over it fairly quickly.'

He paused, and his expression saddened. 'But to me it just didn't seem fair that he died so painfully. That's why I started to drink — to forget the hurt I felt inside. The more I hurt, the more I drank.'

He paused, burying his face in his hands. 'I feel so bitter,' he concluded dejectedly.

Rob thought deeply before replying. 'David, I know what you're going through right now. But hurt and bitterness are things that Jesus understands. Prayer really *does* help.'

Rob looked at David, slumped in the chair. 'You know, of course, some of the things Pam and I have been through.'

'I remember, Rob. It must be easy to look back now and see how good God's been to you.'

Rob sighed. 'You're right. But I can tell you, it wasn't easy at the time. And another thing I've discovered — boozing never solves anything.'

Mr Carman nodded slowly. He knew only too well that things had only seemed worse with each passing day.

'Talking of booze,' continued Rob, 'you're going

to have some apologising to do to the rest of your family for the way you've been today.'

In his own self-pity, this was something Mr Carman hadn't considered until now. But the implications were beginning to hit home.

'Saying sorry to Andy – that isn't going to be easy.'

Rob was taking this conversation slowly and sympathetically. He knew how hard it was for an adult to apologise to a young person. But he also knew how essential it was.

'He'll really respect you for it, David. It takes a lot more guts to ask forgiveness than try and excuse our mistakes.'

Mr Carman thought about this carefully. Why was it that the right way always seemed the hardest? Christians should be used to asking forgiveness. But it never seemed to come any easier.

In the circumstances, he had nothing to lose. All Andy's friends had seen him. There was no longer any point in trying to cover it up.

He made up his mind, and told Rob he'd talk with Andy at the farmhouse before going home.

5

The girls were grouped together around a farm gate admiring the white stallion that Rob had recently purchased.

Claire was bragging about the job she'd been offered at Balcombe stables on Saturday mornings when Rob shouted from the kitchen door.

'Girls, will you ask Andy to come up to the house.'

Emma volunteered to run and fetch him.

When she got there she was amazed to see all three boys standing together and the trike bounding across the field.

'What's happening here?' she wondered as she approached them. But she needed no reply as she saw Bonzo and the punk heading for them at full pelt.

'Hey, you two, get off that trike!' she screamed.

They roared by without even slowing down, laughing and singing as they went.

Then she remembered what she'd really come for.

'Andy, Rob wants to see you.'

Tactfully, she didn't tell him that his dad was at

the house.

'And tell Rob about his trike,' she shouted after him.

Before long, Elaine, Claire and Netsie had come to see what the problem was. They were powerless to do anything. It was all very depressing.

They stared speechless at the punk and Bonzo haring up and down the field with Rob's new miniature trike.

Suddenly, over the crest of the hill came another sound. It was Rob on the larger trike! The gang cheered and shouted.

'Get them, Rob!'

'Go for it, Rob!'

'You two have had it now!'

Rob bounced across the field, full throttle. The punk turned and saw him coming. His face dropped.

He thumped Bonzo on the back. 'Get going, quick!'

Rob was experienced on his trike. To him it was a man's toy, part of a second childhood. He knew the two on their stolen machine would be no match for him on his, much bigger, version.

Bonzo and the punk, for their part, soon realised they weren't going to be able to outpace the larger trike. They raced to the far end of the field, which was bordered by a large ditch.

This seemed to be their lucky day. They came straight to a bridge across the ditch, formed by three large planks laid from one bank to the other.

They drove right across. Then, totally out of character, the punk had a brainwave. He jumped off the trike.

'Come on, let's take out the middle plank; then he

won't be able to get across.'

Together, they lifted the heavy plank up and threw it into the ditch. The little trike sped off across the next field, the riders laughing with glee.

Rob arrived at the bridge too quickly to brake in time. The front wheel went down into the gap. He jumped off the machine and managed to push it on to the field again.

As Rob turned back and drove up the hill, the

punks knew they were safely away. Unexpectedly, Rob turned again and headed back to the bridge.

'What a nutcase,' they thought.

With a mighty heave, Rob lifted the front wheel off the ground and came straight for the bridge, doing a wheelie. He had to be extremely accurate — there was no chance of turning or moving to the left or right. Any error would see him and the trike in the ditch.

The gang held their breath as he drew nearer. Then, suddenly, he was across.

Great cheers went up from the whole gang.

At this point the action disappeared out of their sight.

Rob knew the land. To him, this would be just like rounding up sheep. He steered them, herding them just where he wanted them to go, though they weren't aware of it. In fact, they were driven in a large circle, until they arrived back at the field next to the farm.

This was the moment Rob had been waiting for. Here he would intercept and stop them. But even Rob hadn't fully allowed for their foolhardiness — or maybe the amount of alcohol they had consumed.

Rob hemmed them in so that they had no option but to head straight for the corner where the marsh and pond lay. He figured they would stop when there was no way out.

It may have been that the brakes failed. Perhaps the punk lost all presence of mind. Whatever the reason, the little trike made straight for the pond without even slowing down.

Just in front of the pond was the stump of an old tree. Did Bonzo see it? Or was he too late to avoid it?

The front wheel hit the tree and the two were

catapulted over the handlebars. They landed with two great splashes in the pond, causing great consternation to the resident ducks, who left in disgust.

The gang exploded into fits of laughter. The sight of those two threatening characters sitting up to their chests in muddy water, with weeds and grime over their hair and faces, was just too much. They couldn't control themselves.

After spitting all the dirty water from his mouth and wringing out his ears, Bonzo stood up.

'That's it. I thought you said this was a quiet place,' he seethed angrily to the punk.

The punk just sat there, too livid to move.

Shouting to no one in particular, he vented his anger: 'I don't like kids. I don't just not like them, I detest them. I *hate kids*!'

This outburst had no effect on the gang except to send them into further peals of laughter.

The punk stood up, lost his balance and promptly sat down again. He thumped the water with his fist. Bonzo pulled him out and they squelched off across the field, still airing their complaints loudly.

'This your idea of fun, is it?' Bonzo complained, their friendship coming under strain.

'It's your fault. I came here for a nice quiet day bullying kids and what do we get? Being chased by a madman at a hundred miles an hour on a scooter.'

Bonzo was content to let him go on.

'I ain't comin' back here again . . . . I'm goin' home . . . . I hate you.' Their complaints faded into the distance.

'Come on,' Rob grinned. 'Let's go back to the farm. Pam should be ready with tea. And I expect Andy and his dad'll be glad to see us by now.'

The boys helped pull the small trike back the right way up and the three of them jumped on. The girls clambered on to Rob's trike and they all headed up to the farm, into the wind and towards the appetising smell of warm scones.